Bookworms Club

Reading Circles

Teacher's Handbook

Third Edition

EDITOR: MARK FURR

For use with all Bookworms Club Students' Books

Series Editor, Oxford Bookworms Library: Jennifer Bassett

OXFORD

OXFORD
UNIVERSITY PRESS

Great Clarendon Street, Oxford, OX2 6DP, United Kingdom

Oxford University Press is a department of the University of Oxford.
It furthers the University's objective of excellence in research, scholarship,
and education by publishing worldwide. Oxford is a registered trade
mark of Oxford University Press in the UK and in certain other countries

ISBN: 978 0 19 472010 6

Printed in China

This book is printed on paper from certified and well-managed sources

AN AWARD-WINNING SERIES

The British Council Innovation Awards (the ELTons) are offered
to outstanding language learning resources and initiatives which use
innovative ideas to help learners of English achieve their goals.

Bookworms Club Reading Circles
Teacher's and Student's Books (*Bronze*, *Silver*, and *Gold*) were
the winners of a **British Council Innovation Award** in 2008.

The **Language Learner Literature Awards** are conferred each year by the
Extensive Reading Foundation on graded readers in English that are selected
for their outstanding overall quality and likely enduring appeal.

Bookworms Club Gold
was a finalist for the **Language Learner Literature Awards** in 2008.

CONTENTS

Answers to all Bookworms Club Story Activities are available
on the website <www.oup.com/elt/teacher/readingcircles>

Pages marked PHOTOCOPIABLE are also available
on the website <www.oup.com/elt/teacher/readingcircles>

ACKNOWLEDGEMENTS

As Editor of the *Bookworms Club* series, I would like to acknowledge the following people for both their support of the project and their contributions to the series. First, I must acknowledge the work of Harvey Daniels and his team of teachers and researchers in Chicago, USA. In 1994, Daniels published *Literature Circles: Voice and Choice in Book Clubs & Reading Groups*. In this work, he introduced both the theory and practice of using classroom-based reading groups in L1 classes. Daniels and his colleagues laid the foundation for the current development of Reading Circles for L2 students. Next, Paul Riley and Robert Habbick, two strong proponents of extensive reading in the Asia ELT market, helped to fan the flames of Reading Circles in Japan. They provided a number of venues at which to introduce L2 Reading Circles to teachers, and they offered a number of great suggestions along the way. And thanks to Bill Bowler for sharing some very insightful comments on an early draft of the publishing proposal. I must also acknowledge Pamela Bostelmann for her TESOL Arabia (2002) presentation on Literature Circles. Pamela's presentation served as my introduction to classroom-based reading groups. Tina Ferrato, my partner, and the hardest-working teacher I have ever met, contributed to this work in more ways than I can articulate. Tina is a fierce proponent of extensive reading, and it was her interest which first hooked me on the use of graded readers in ELT. Finally, I must thank Jennifer Bassett for her work on this project. Without Jennifer, this series simply would not have been published. She has been the master jeweller, teaching a newly-appointed apprentice how to take a very rough gem and to slowly chip away at it until it is ready to be faceted and polished.

Mark Furr
Hawaii, June 2006

Why use Reading Circles?

In all cultures, over thousands of years, people have been fascinated by a good story – and language students are no exception. And a good story is at the heart of every Reading Circle.

Reading Circles combine, in a natural way, the skills of reading, writing, speaking, and listening. They help motivate students to acquire both the habits of reading extensively and of working autonomously. They accomplish this by providing two things that are often lacking in many oral communication courses: material that is both comprehensible and interesting to talk about, and a framework which makes having a real discussion in English an achievable goal for students.

Once students are engaged by a story, they are willing to write carefully in order to be prepared for their group discussions; to speak in English almost all of the time while in their groups; to eagerly point to passages within a text in order to support their arguments; and to question each other in order to establish what the text really means. There are many reasons to use Reading Circles in the classroom, but the best way to discover them is to try Reading Circles for yourself.

What are Reading Circles?

Reading Circles are small groups of students who meet in the classroom to talk about stories. These groups allow language learners to have enjoyable, interesting discussions in English. In a Reading Circle, each student plays a different role in the discussion. The six main roles are:

**Discussion Leader   Summarizer   Connector
Word Master   Passage Person   Culture Collector**

To prepare for their roles, each student completes a Role Sheet. The Role Sheets break reading down into smaller sub-skills with each student focusing closely on one way of encountering the text. The students read the story from their given perspective (role) outside the class. Then they are brought together in the Reading Circle, where they use their Role Sheets as prompts for discussion, and during this process of discussion the parts become whole.

Key Features of Reading Circles

Reading Circles are reading and discussion groups which are very much student centred. The teacher's role is to provide students with a framework for success.

1 Teachers select reading material appropriate for their student population

Reading Circles ask language learners to have 'real-life', meaningful discussions about the stories that they have read. So it is important for the teacher to choose appropriately graded reading texts, which students can read *without* using a dictionary.

2 Small temporary groups are formed in the classroom

Five to six students in a Reading Circle works best. At first, teachers should manage the groups so that each group has one or two confident students who are willing to take a risk with something new.

3 Different groups read the same text

There are a number of advantages if each group reads the same story. First, it is much easier for the teacher to monitor the progress of the discussion groups. Secondly, using the story text as core material, it is possible to assign a number of different extension activities, including oral presentations and poster sessions. Group projects and extension activities are ways to evaluate students for their Reading Circles work.

4 Groups meet on a regular, predictable schedule to discuss their reading

This is a crucial aspect to the success of Reading Circles. Reading Circles require some student training time, so a teacher must be willing to commit to several stories and rounds of discussion if there are to be positive results.

5 Students use written notes to guide both their reading and their discussion

The Role Sheets (described on pages 8 and 9) prompt each member of the group to read a story from a different perspective, and to make notes in English in order to prepare for a group discussion based on their reading. In this way, students are learning that there are a number of different reasons for reading, and that there are also varying perspectives on any given text.

6 Discussion topics come from the students

It is important to allow students to generate the topics for discussion. These are not classes in literary criticism, but informal discussions about stories. The Role Sheets provide the help needed for students to find interesting topics.

7 Group meetings aim to be open, natural conversations about stories

Students are encouraged to share their opinions about the texts which are read for Reading Circles, so not all of the discussion will be serious.

8 The teacher serves as a facilitator, not a group member or instructor

Teachers need to step back and allow students to assume responsibility for guiding the Reading Circle discussions. Some teachers may not be used to this, but since students complete the Role Sheets in advance, and know the roles that they are to play in the group, teachers must allow this process to work naturally.

9 A spirit of playfulness and fun pervades the room

Of course, if Reading Circles are not fun, then we are simply repackaging the types of lessons which students tell us that they hate. The goal of Reading Circles is clear and simple – to promote informal talk about great stories!

Getting Started with Reading Circles

Material Selection

In Reading Circles students are asked not only to read stories, but also to discuss them in English. So it is important for the teacher to choose appropriately graded reading texts that students can read without using a dictionary. Here are some good 'rules of thumb' for students to find their reading level:

- There should be no more than 2 to 3 unknown words per page.
- The learner is reading 8 to 10 lines of text or more per minute.
- The learner understands almost all of what they are reading with few pauses.

More advice on assessing the suitability of texts for extensive reading can be found in *Getting the most out of your Readers* by Rob Waring on the website <www.oup.com/elt/gradedreading>. It is usually a good idea to begin with a graded text that is one level *below* the student's current reading level. This helps to boost their confidence and enjoyment of the activity.

Introducing the Role Sheets

The magic behind Reading Circles lies in the Role Sheets, which guide learners through their reading, and make it both easy and manageable to prepare for discussions in English about stories they have read. So it is important to spend some class time introducing the Role Sheets clearly to students. These steps are recommended:

1 Put students into groups of five or six. (These will become the first Reading Circle groups.) Try to make sure that there are at least two confident students in each group.

2 Give each student a set of the six Role Sheets from pages 14–19, or from the website <www.oup.com/elt/teacher/readingcircles>. There are also small versions in the students' books, but the larger sheets allow more space for students to write notes during the introductory session.

3 It is often a good idea to introduce the first five roles now, and wait until the second or third session of Reading Circles before introducing the sixth role, Culture Collector.

4 Present each role one at a time (using the notes on the next two pages), pausing after each one. Allow students time to talk among themselves in their groups, to consolidate their understanding of the role. Encourage them to write notes on the Role Sheets, which they can keep and refer to later when they are assigned a particular role.

5 After the five (or six) roles have been presented, give students a photocopy of the Role Sheet Examples (pages 20–21). Invite them to write down a few questions about the roles. These questions can then be put on the board, and teachers can either answer them or elicit answers from other groups in the class.

Here are suggestions for presenting each role to students. On the left are the 'job descriptions' from the Role Sheets which the students will be looking at; on the right are some notes giving extra information or emphasizing important points.

Student's Role Sheets

The Discussion Leader's job is to ...
- read the story twice, and prepare at least five general questions about it.
- ask one or two questions to start the Reading Circle discussion.
- make sure that everyone has a chance to speak and joins in the discussion.
- call on each member to present their prepared role information.
- guide the discussion and keep it going.

Notes for the Teacher

*It is a good idea to arrange for a confident student to act as **Discussion Leader** for the first few sessions.*
1 When asking the first questions, the DL calls on each student at least once, so that everyone speaks before the other roles are presented.
2 After each role is presented, the DL asks a new general question and calls on each student to answer, so that everyone in the group has many chances to speak.
3 The DL encourages people to ask questions at any time in the discussion.
4 The DL does not act as a teacher, but as a discussion guide.

The Summarizer's job is to ...
- read the story and make notes about the characters, events, and ideas.
- find the key points that everyone must know to understand and remember the story.
- retell the story in a short summary (one or two minutes) in your own words.
- talk about your summary to the group, using your writing to help you.

*The **Summarizer** should focus only on the main events of the story.*
1 Emphasize that the Summarizer retells the story in their own words, and does not copy too much from the story text.
2 The Summarizer should not read a prepared text to the group, but give a spoken summary, using the notes from their Role Sheet as a guide.
3 In the first discussions, it can be a good idea for the Summarizer to give their summary once, pause for a minute, then give the summary a second time.

The Connector's job is to ...
- read the story twice, and look for connections between the story and the world outside.
- make notes about at least two possible connections to your own experiences, or to the experiences of friends and family, or to real-life events.
- tell the group about the connections and ask for their comments or questions.
- ask the group if they can think of any connections themselves.

*Students can find the **Connector** role challenging at first, so it is a good idea if a confident student is given this role for the first few discussions.*
1 Emphasize that students can focus on characters as well as events in the story.
2 In some kinds of story (for example, mystery, horror, adventure), students will rarely have had similar experiences. But they can still find connections with the feelings or thoughts of characters in the story (for example, fear, shock, guilt, excitement).
3 Connectors should present one connection, then ask the group for questions before moving on to the next connection on their Role Sheet.

The Word Master's job is to ...

- read the story, and look for words or short phrases that are new or difficult to understand, or that are important in the story.
- choose five words (only five) that you think are important for this story.
- explain the meanings of these five words in simple English to the group.
- tell the group why these words are important for understanding this story.

*The **Word Master** can ask other group members to read aloud the sentences where the words appear. This allows everyone more speaking time and helps the group to focus on the words in context.*

1 Make sure that students understand they should look for words that are important in the story – they do not have to choose unknown words.

2 Students should use an English-to-English learner's dictionary to define new words.

3 Encourage students to look for special uses of common words and to ask questions such as, 'What do you think _____ means here?' Or 'Why does the writer repeat the word _____ eight times in the first two pages of this story?'

The Passage Person's job is to ...

- read the story, and find important, interesting, or difficult passages.
- make notes about at least three passages that are important for the plot, or that explain the characters, or that have very interesting or powerful language.
- read each passage to the group, or ask another group member to read it.
- ask the group one or two questions about each passage.

*The **Passage Person** can also ask other group members to read aloud the selected passages, allowing everyone more speaking time and helping the group to focus on the context in which the passages occur.*

1 Remind students that they do not have to choose passages containing the main events in a story. Interesting descriptions, characters' thoughts, or pieces of dialogue often provide good material for group discussion.

2 Students must remember to give their reasons for choosing a particular passage.

3 Encourage the Passage Person to ask the group for help with any passages they find puzzling. Some of the best discussion occurs while students are trying to work out the meaning of difficult passages together.

The Culture Collector's job is to ...

- read the story, and look for both differences and similarities between your own culture and the culture found in the story.
- make notes about two or three passages that show these cultural points.
- read each passage to the group, or ask another group member to read it.
- ask the group some questions about these, and any other cultural points in the story.

*The **Culture Collector** role is probably the most challenging one, and it may be best not to introduce this role until the groups have read and discussed at least one story. It is also a good idea if a confident student acts as Culture Collector the first time the role is used.*

1 Explain that 'your culture' includes your background, your customs and traditions, your everyday life.

2 Encourage the Culture Collector to ask the group for help in understanding puzzling cultural issues in the story.

3 This role and the Connector role are similar. Both look for connections: the Connector finds connections with personal experience; the Culture Collector compares and contrasts cultures, and finds cross-cultural connections.

Reading and Role Sheet Preparation

After the Role Sheet introductory session, here are some other useful things to do to help prepare students for Reading Circles. (See also the Frequently Asked Questions opposite.)

1 Reading Schedule

Each student fills in their own copy of a Reading Circles Schedule (page 13). They write the story title, the names of their group members, and the role each member will play during the discussion meeting.

2 In class or out of class

With younger or lower-level students, both the reading and the Role Sheet preparation can be done in class. However, students usually read the entire short story and complete their Role Sheet, in English, as homework, to prepare for the discussion meeting. If students are working on their Role Sheets out of class, remind them of the advice given on the Reading Circles Roles page in their students' book – *Read, think, connect, ask … and connect.*

3 Accessible language

Students must understand that their Role Sheets will be used as notes for discussion, so they must use vocabulary and structures which their classmates will understand. Advise students not to use a dictionary while completing their Role Sheets unless it is an English-to-English learner's dictionary.

4 Rehearsal

Encourage students, before coming to class, to practise reading aloud to themselves their Role Sheet notes. Emphasize that their written notes are to help with the discussion.

5 Absent group members

In some teaching situations, it is a good idea to tell students that even if they are absent on the day of the Reading Circle meeting, they still must have their work ready, and must pass it to another group member who can present it for them in class. Making students responsible for their roles, whether they are in class or not, promotes not only student responsibility but also a very high attendance rate. When students realize that they have to complete the assignment whether they are present or not, they often decide that it is easier to come to class and participate than to arrange to send in their homework by proxy.

6 Role badges

If appropriate, and if students wish, they can make role badges for themselves, using the photocopiable role icons on the last page of this book. The role icon badges are also on the last page of the students' books and the website <www.oup.com/elt/teacher/readingcircles>.

Group Discussions

Discussion in small groups of five or six may be new for many students, and for the first Reading Circle session, it is a good idea to allow only thirty to forty minutes of discussion time. This should be enough for each group to go through all the roles and have time for follow-up questions and comments. The goal is to finish before the students have exhausted their enthusiasm for discussion so that they will be motivated to try Reading Circles again!

Frequently Asked Questions (FAQs)

1 My class doesn't divide evenly into groups of 5 or 6. How do I organize it?

If the groups are larger, two different students can take the role of Connector or Passage Person. In other words, there can be two Connectors and/or Passage Persons in a group (they work independently, not as partners). If there are not enough students in a group, the Discussion Leader can also act as Summarizer.

2 Who allocates the roles? Do students take a different role in turn? Can students choose their own roles?

For the first Reading Circle discussion in a class, it is recommended that the teacher allocate the roles. For subsequent stories, new groups are formed, and students may then be allowed to choose roles in their new circles. However, students should always be asked to take a different role for each new story.

3 What age groups are Reading Circles aimed at?

Reading Circles can be used with language learners of almost any age, from junior high school right through to college and university level, and in vocational training and adult education.

4 How long will one complete round of Reading Circles take?

The first round of Reading Circles will take longer than subsequent rounds, as introducing the roles and a general introduction to Reading Circles usually takes about 35 to 45 minutes in class. After the first round, it need not take more than 10 or 15 minutes to form new groups, allocate roles, and remind students of Reading Circle procedures. Students should plan on between 30 and 60 minutes for reading the story and role sheet preparation, either inside or outside the class. Discussions in class should run to about 40 minutes.

5 Can students in Reading Circles choose which stories they want to read?

No, at least not at first. Asking students to have purposeful, small-group discussions in English about the stories they have read is a complex undertaking for both students and teachers alike. With each group reading the same story, it is much easier for the teacher to monitor the progress of the discussion groups and to make adjustments where necessary. Also, the stories in the *Bookworms Club* series are organized so that students read and discuss progressively longer texts, and the last stories in each book move up one stage in the Bookworms grading system, so it is best to read and discuss the stories in the order presented.

6 When should students do the activities after each story in the students' book?

Since the *Bookworms Club* series does not gloss words outside the headword list for the level, students should read the story straight through without stopping, and then complete the *Word Focus* activity. If reading time is allocated in class, the *Word Focus* activity can be done in class in pairs. The *Story Focus* activities are designed to model the close-reading skills needed to complete the Role Sheets, so students can be asked to complete these activities before working on the Role Sheets, either in class or as part of their preparation at home.

Using Reading Circles with Longer Stories

The *Bookworms Club* series contains collections of short stories and support materials especially designed for use with Reading Circles. It is also possible to use longer texts, such as full-length Bookworms. The procedures for forming groups and introducing the roles remain the same, but there are some important differences to keep in mind.

Key Differences

1 Choosing the level

It is very important for the teacher to select an appropriately graded text, and a full-length story should be *one level below* the students' current reading level. Students are being asked to read, make notes, and discuss a larger quantity of text, so the teacher must make sure that students are able to process these longer texts without reaching the point of frustration.

2 Chunking the story

With a longer story, students are assigned a specific number of pages to read and asked to prepare one role for this 'chunk' of the text. Usually, ten to fifteen pages of assigned reading, or one or two chapters, is a manageable amount. Look for natural breaks in a story, at chapter ends or other divisions in the text. It can be helpful to look at the *While-Reading* activities (found at the back of each full-length Bookworm), which often chunk the story into groups of chapters at strategic points in the plot. Prediction activities – speculating about developments in plot or character – can be a useful way of carrying the story forward from one Reading Circle meeting to the next. However, always remind students *not* to read ahead of the assigned section, otherwise discussions can become very confusing, with some students knowing more of the story than others.

3 Rotating the roles

Students should rotate through the different roles for each meeting discussing different sections of the story. A student who acts as Discussion Leader for the first assignment of reading (for example, chapters 1 and 2) might then play the role of Connector for the second session (chapters 3 and 4). This change of focus and activity helps to keep students interested in the reading, and encourages them to bring fresh perspectives to each meeting.

Reminders

Whichever texts are used, the essence of Reading Circles remains the same. It is enabling learners to have meaningful, interesting discussions in English. The teacher's role is to

- make sure that students are reading stories at appropriate language levels for them
- present the roles clearly so that students know what is expected of them
- assign a manageable quantity of text for Role Sheet preparation
- then step back, and allow Reading Circles to work their magic!

PHOTOCOPIABLE

BOOKWORMS CLUB

READING CIRCLES SCHEDULE

	1st meeting	2nd meeting	3rd meeting	4th meeting	5th meeting	6th meeting	7th meeting
DATE							
STORY TITLE							
ROLE	NAMES	NAMES	NAMES	NAMES	NAMES	NAMES	NAMES
DISCUSSION LEADER							
SUMMARIZER							
CONNECTOR							
WORD MASTER							
PASSAGE PERSON							
CULTURE COLLECTOR							

READING CIRCLES ROLE SHEETS
In Reading Circles, each student has their own role. The six roles are usually Discussion Leader, Summarizer, Connector, Word Master,
Passage Person, Culture Collector. These role sheets will help you prepare for your Reading Circle discussions in the classroom.

Discussion Leader

STORY: _____

NAME: _____

The Discussion Leader's job is to ...

• read the story twice, and prepare at least five general questions about it.

• ask one or two questions to start the Reading Circle discussion.

• make sure that everyone has a chance to speak and joins in the discussion.

• call on each member to present their prepared role information.

• guide the discussion and keep it going.

Usually the best discussion questions come from your own thoughts, feelings, and questions as you read. (What surprised you, made you smile, made you feel sad?) Write down your questions as soon as you have finished reading. It is best to use your own questions, but you can also use some of the ideas at the bottom of this page.

MY QUESTIONS:

1 _____

— _____

— _____

— _____

— _____

— _____

— _____

— _____

— _____

— _____

— _____

— _____

— _____

— _____

Other general ideas:

• Questions about the characters (*like / not like them, true to life / not true to life ...*?)

• Questions about the theme (*friendship, romance, parents/children, ghosts ...*?)

• Questions about the ending (*surprising, expected, liked it / did not like it ...*?)

• Questions about what will happen next. (These can also be used for a longer story.)

Summarizer

STORY: _____

NAME: _____

(**S**)

The Summarizer's job is to ...

• read the story and make notes about the characters, events, and ideas.

• find the key points that everyone must know to understand and remember the story.

• retell the story in a short summary (one or two minutes) in your own words.

• talk about your summary to the group, using your writing to help you.

Your reading circle will find your summary very useful, because it will help to remind them of the plot and the characters in the story. You may need to read the story more than once to make a good summary, and you may need to repeat it to the group a second time.

MY KEY POINTS:

Main events:_____

_____

_____

_____

_____

Characters:_____

_____

_____

_____

_____

MY SUMMARY:

_____

_____

_____

_____

_____

_____

_____

_____

_____

_____

Connector

STORY: _____

NAME: _____

The Connector's job is to ...

• read the story twice, and look for connections between the story and the world outside.

• make notes about at least two possible connections to your own experiences, or to the experiences of friends and family, or to real-life events.

• tell the group about the connections and ask for their comments or questions.

• ask the group if they can think of any connections themselves.

These questions will help you think about connections while you are reading.

Events: Has anything similar ever happened to you, or to someone you know? Does anything in the story remind you of events in the real world? For example, events you have read about in newspapers, or heard about on television news programmes.

Characters: Do any of them remind you of people you know? How? Why? Have you ever had the same thoughts or feelings as these characters have? Do you know anybody who thinks, feels, behaves like that?

MY CONNECTIONS:

1 _____

_____

_____

_____

_____

_____

_____

_____

_____

_____

_____

_____

_____

_____

_____

_____

_____

READING CIRCLES ROLE SHEETS

In Reading Circles, each student has their own role. The six roles are usually Discussion Leader, Summarizer, Connector, Word Master, Passage Person, Culture Collector. These role sheets will help you prepare for your Reading Circle discussions in the classroom.

Word Master

STORY: _____

NAME: _____

W

The Word Master's job is to ...

- read the story, and look for words or short phrases that are new or difficult to understand, or that are important in the story.
- choose five words (only five) that you think are important for this story.
- explain the meanings of these five words in simple English to the group.
- tell the group why these words are important for understanding this story.

Your five words do not have to be new or unknown words. Look for words in the story that really stand out in some way. These may be words that are:

- repeated often
- used in an unusual way
- important to the meaning of the story

MY WORDS	MEANING OF THE WORD	REASON FOR CHOOSING THE WORD
PAGE _____ LINE _____		
PAGE _____ LINE _____		
PAGE _____ LINE _____		
PAGE _____ LINE _____		
PAGE _____ LINE _____		

Passage Person

STORY: _____

NAME: _____

The Passage Person's job is to ...

• read the story, and find important, interesting, or difficult passages.

• make notes about at least three passages that are important for the plot, or that explain the characters, or that have very interesting or powerful language.

• read each passage to the group, or ask another group member to read it.

• ask the group one or two questions about each passage.

A passage is usually one paragraph, but sometimes it can be just one or two sentences, or perhaps a piece of dialogue. You might choose a passage to discuss because it is:

• important   • informative   • surprising   • funny   • confusing   • well-written

MY PASSAGES:

PAGE _____ LINES _____

REASONS FOR CHOOSING THE PASSAGE

_____

_____

_____

_____

_____

QUESTIONS ABOUT THE PASSAGE

_____

_____

_____

_____

_____

PAGE _____ LINES _____

REASONS FOR CHOOSING THE PASSAGE

_____

_____

_____

_____

_____

QUESTIONS ABOUT THE PASSAGE

_____

_____

_____

_____

_____

PAGE _____ LINES _____

REASONS FOR CHOOSING THE PASSAGE

_____

_____

_____

_____

_____

QUESTIONS ABOUT THE PASSAGE

_____

_____

_____

_____

_____

Culture Collector

STORY: _____

NAME: _____

The Culture Collector's job is to ...

• read the story, and look for both differences and similarities between your own culture and the culture found in the story.

• make notes about two or three passages that show these cultural points.

• read each passage to the group, or ask another group member to read it.

• ask the group some questions about these, and any other cultural points in the story.

Here are some questions to help you think about cultural differences.

Theme: What is the theme of this story (for example, getting married, meeting a ghost, murder, unhappy children)? Is this an important theme in your own culture? Do people think about this theme in the same way, or differently?

People: Do characters in this story say or do things that people never say or do in your culture? Do they say or do some things that everybody in the world says or does?

MY CULTURAL COLLECTION (differences and similarities):

1 **PAGE** _____ **LINES** _____ : _____

_____

_____

_____

_____

_____

_____

2 **PAGE** _____ **LINES** _____ : _____

_____

_____

_____

_____

_____

_____

MY CULTURAL QUESTIONS:

1 _____

2 _____

3 _____

Role Sheet Examples

💬 Discussion Leader   STORY: The Five Orange Pips

MY QUESTIONS:

1 Do you like detective stories? Why or why not?
2 Imagine that you are John Openshaw, and you get the five orange pips in a letter. How would you feel? What would you do next?
3 Did anything in this story surprise you?

Ⓢ Summarizer   STORY: Netty Sargent and the House

MY KEY POINTS:

Main events: _The young, pretty girl's uncle dies before he signs the paper to give her a house. The girl tells a lie and puts her dead uncle in a chair. She moves his hand to sign the papers, and the agent watches._

Characters: _Netty is a pretty, young girl. Netty lives with her old uncle. He is very ill. Jasper is Netty's boyfriend, but he doesn't love her so much. He wants to get the old man's house._

MY SUMMARY:

Netty really wants to marry Jasper. But Jasper says he won't marry her if she loses her uncle's house. Netty's uncle doesn't like Jasper. So he waits to sign the papers to give the house to Netty. Finally, Netty's uncle says he will sign the papers, but he dies before the agent comes with them. Then, Netty puts her dead uncle in a chair. And she moves her dead uncle's hand to sign the papers. The agent watches, and Netty gets the house. But Jasper is a bad husband.

Ⓦ Word Master   STORY: The Christmas Presents© OXFORD UNIVERSITY PRESS

MY WORDS	MEANING OF THE WORD	REASON FOR CHOOSING THE WORD
One dollar and eighty-seven cents. PAGE _4_ LINE _1 - 8_	This is a small amount of money in the U.S.	This tells us how poor they are and shows us that Della thinks she needs to buy something as a gift for her husband.
curls PAGE _6_ LINE _14_	These are little rings of hair.	Della was worried about her curls. We think curls are cute. So I don't understand why she was worried. Perhaps, in the story's time, only straight hair was beautiful.

Ⓒ Connector   **STORY:** *The Christmas Presents*

MY CONNECTIONS:

1 I was moved by this story because I remember that giving a present to someone is not important. But our heart and mind is important when we try to give a present. When I was an elementary school student, I gave my father a present. I carefully made a very small stuffed toy cat. I sewed it with felt. Then, I wrote a short letter to my father and put it into the cat's mouth. "Finished, I did it." But when I saw my workmanship again, it looked ugly and careless. The next day was my father's birthday. I gave the failure to him, but he was very pleased! I couldn't understand it. But as the years passed, the more I understood it. I am much older, but my father still has my ugly cat. I noticed that he received not my present, but my heart at that time. This is the same feeling that Jim and Della have when they get the presents that are useless.

▤ Passage Person   **STORY:** *The Tell-Tale Heart*

PASSAGE: I could see it clearly, a horrible, pale blue eye that turned my blood cold. I could see nothing of the man's face or body, just his eye.

MY PASSAGES:

PAGE ___57___ LINES <u>27, 28, 29</u>

REASONS FOR CHOOSING THE PASSAGE
This is interesting because it is easy to imagine the main character's fear and the silence of the scene.

QUESTIONS ABOUT THE PASSAGE
Why does the main character fear only the old man's eye? Is it a magic eye? Is it very ugly? Does the old man have a disease?

↻ Culture Collector   **STORY:** *The Joy Luck Club*

MY CULTURAL COLLECTION (differences and similarities):

1 PAGE ___94___ LINES ___6-10___ :   In my primary school days, we had the "open day" when our parents visit our classes. A friend of mine didn't want her mother to come to school. She said that her mother looked ugly and was shorter than the other mothers. She never wanted anyone to know. I remembered this because the Chinese-American daughter in this story is also ashamed of her mother because of her appearance. Like me, my friend is Japanese, and she had the same feeling as the daughter in the story. Maybe it is an Asian idea.

2 PAGE _____ LINES _____ : _____

      PHOTOCOPIABLE

Expanding the Circle

The Reading Circle Role Sheets provide a framework for language learners to discuss a common text in English, but that is only the beginning, because at the heart of every Reading Circle, there is a great story. Stories cross boundaries of geography, culture, theme, and time; they create alternative realities that intersect with the real world, reflect it, and comment on it, obliquely or directly. The Reading Circles discussion format can be expanded to include many different activities that continue to explore the story. Here are just a few ideas:

An Illustrator Role asks students, singly or in pairs, to illustrate a central image, theme, or metaphor in a story. Illustrations can be in the form of sketches, cartoons, collages, diagrams, or any type of graphic. Illustrations can be presented to the group without comment, so that the group has a chance to discuss different interpretations.

A Background Investigator Role asks students, working in groups of two or three, to do additional research following the group discussion, in order to find background information on some aspect of a story. For example, students might be asked to look into the historical accuracy of a story, or to find information about the place where the story is set, or about the social customs that were common in that country at that time.

Mini-Presentations by teachers on authors, or cultural or historical points from the story. Once students have discussed a story, and it has captured their interest, the stage has been set for meaningful work on listening comprehension, and teachers who want to integrate listening skills into their Reading Circles classes can use these presentations, or mini-lectures, to provide listening and note-taking practice. A good mini-lecture in English can reinforce topic vocabulary raised during the group discussions. Mini-lectures range from 15 to 25 minutes depending on the language level of the students.

Mini-Presentations by students on biographical information about selected authors. Students will need to do some additional research for these presentations, so it is best if they work in pairs, threes, or entire Reading Circle groups. Presentations can be made as oral presentations to the class, or in the form of poster sessions. These presentations range from 10 to 20 minutes.

Poster Session – students work together in their Reading Circles to create a poster illustrating one or more aspects of a story, such as the theme, author, or background of the story, then present their posters to the class. See the page opposite for a detailed guide to this activity.

Plot Pyramid Activity – each Reading Circle group creates a plot diagram for a story they have just discussed, and then presents their findings to the class. See page 24 for a detailed guide to this activity.

Reading Circles Poster Sessions

Poster sessions offer an enjoyable and interesting way to expand on Reading Circle group discussions. Students enjoy the creative aspect of assembling the posters, and teachers can use both the posters and short oral presentations as ways of evaluating students for their Reading Circles work. Poster Sessions ask students to practise some basic research and oral presentation skills, so teachers should tailor the complexity of these tasks to fit both their course objectives and student population. Also, it is best if students complete at least two full Reading Circle sessions (role preparation and group discussion) before trying this activity.

Poster Session Guide

1 For the first poster session in a class, it is best to have all the groups make posters about the same story. This serves two purposes. First, when all the groups are working on the same story, it is much easier for the teacher to assist students in finding information for their posters. Next, students generally find it interesting to see posters about the same story created from the different perspectives of other Reading Circle groups in the class.

2 Ask students to look at the Poster Activity pages in the student book. Read the instructions together and look at the poster graphic. The first time, it may work best to have different groups focus on just one or two of the categories suggested there. Or teachers can leave the activity completely open, allowing each group to choose whichever categories they like.

3 Teachers may ask students to find additional information to create their posters, or they may supply materials to each group themselves. Students should be encouraged to look for pictures and graphics as well as text, and if they do research outside the class, it is a good idea to set up research teams of two or three students within each Reading Circle.

4 The research teams work independently, and when they bring their materials to class, each Reading Circle will have at least two different sets of information from their research teams. The full group then decides how to use this information to create the poster.

5 Students create their posters in class. Give each group one large piece of poster paper, and ensure they have glue, marker pens, and other materials needed. Students can be asked in advance to bring these items, or teachers can supply them.

6 Each group makes notes which they will use when doing their poster presentations.

7 The posters are put up around the classroom, and Reading Circle members take turns presenting their posters to small groups of classmates. There can be five or six mini-presentations happening at the same time, with each group rotating pairs of presenters as students move around the room to watch different mini-presentations.

Plotting the Pyramid

This activity gives students an opportunity to experience a story from a new perspective. After they have read and discussed a story in their circles, students will already know the story quite well and will be familiar with the characters and events. The Plot Pyramid activity then asks them to examine closely the plot of the story and to break it down into five distinct parts.

The activity also provides ways of evaluating students for their Reading Circles work. Teachers can evaluate both the Plot Pyramids created by each group and the short presentations about the pyramids which students may give in class. However, it is best if students complete at least two full Reading Circle sessions (role preparation and group discussion) before trying this activity.

Guidelines for Plotting the Pyramid

1 Ask students to look at the Pyramid Activity pages in the student book. In class, read through the descriptions for each of the five parts of the pyramid.

2 Then use examples from a recently read story to illustrate each part of the pyramid. As a whole class activity, ask each Reading Circle several questions to help them identify one part of the pyramid. Allow the groups a few minutes to come up with possible answers, and then, using their answers, plot a simple pyramid on the board. This can then be used as an example, or model, for the story the students are currently working on.

3 Give each group a photocopy of the graphic for Plotting the Pyramid on the page opposite.

4 Read through the section called *How to Plot the Pyramid* in the student book.

5 Explain to students that for each part of the pyramid, there may be different possible answers, according to their own understanding of the story. This is especially the case for the **Complication**, the **Rising Action**, and the **Climax**. Tell students that they need to be story detectives, who look for clues and find reasons for identifying particular passages as the parts of the pyramid.

6 In their Reading Circles, students work together to find each part of the pyramid and to complete the sentences on the pyramid activity sheet.

7 The groups, in turn, draw their pyramids on the board, and then explain each point to the class. There may be interesting variations in the pyramids, and teachers might encourage each Reading Circle in the audience to ask one question after each pyramid presentation.

This activity can also be done as a Poster Session. See points 5 to 7 in the Poster Sessions guide on the previous page.

STORY TITLE

4 Climax

This is when _____

_____

This is the Climax because _____

_____

_____

3 Rising Action

The two most important points are

_____

_____

They are important because _____

_____

_____

_____

CLIMAX

2 Complication

This is when _____

This is the Complication because _____

_____

_____

RISING ACTION

EXPOSITION

RESOLUTION

COMPLICATION

1 Exposition

The important points are _____

_____

_____

_____

_____

_____

5 Resolution

This is when _____

_____

This is the Resolution because _____

_____

_____

_____

Bookworms Club Story Activities

Each story in the Bookworms Club series has support material to help students in their preparation for their Reading Circle roles. The material consists of:

Story introductions	Word Focus activities
About the Authors	Story Focus activities

It can be a good idea for students to keep a Reading Circles notebook, in which they write their answers to all activities, including notes used for Expansion Activities. This has several advantages:

• First, with the Word Focus activities, students are recording the vocabulary outside the Bookworms level for that story, and which therefore might be new to them. This serves as a useful reference for their Role Sheet preparation.

• Next, since the Story Focus activities model the close reading required in the more challenging roles, students are generating examples of the type of work that will be needed when completing the Role Sheets.

• Finally, student notebooks can be valuable for assessment purposes. The teacher can quickly circulate through the class, looking at the notebooks and recording whether or not students have completed the activities. The notebooks also act as portfolios of student work during a Reading Circle cycle, and assessment of these portfolios can be a way of giving students credit for some of their Reading Circles work.

Story introductions

1 These short introductions are designed to help the reader enter the world of the story, to give a preview of what might come, and to arouse curiosity as to how the story might develop. The introduction might give some information about time and place, the setting of the story, and will usually hint at the theme and the atmosphere of the story. And it might also mention one or two characters, and the dilemmas or difficulties that those characters might face.

2 When students are reading the story at home and preparing for their role, always encourage them to read the story introduction first. This will help to activate their predictive skills when reading. They might also mark what they believe is the most important piece of information in the introduction. This ensures that they have a solid entry point into the story, and helps to prepare them for the type of close reading required for completing their Role Sheets.

Word Focus activities

1 These are intended to help students with the vocabulary items in the story that might be unknown, or that are particularly crucial for understanding the story. They are straightforward, traditional

exercises such as crosswords, matching words with definitions, and gap-filling in short passages. They are meant to be done quickly, and their aim is simply to help students become familiar with the topic vocabulary, so that they can use these words confidently in discussion.

2 The Bookworms Club series does not gloss words outside the Bookworms list for the level, so it is a good idea to check that students have completed the Word Focus activity. The goal is simply to make sure that they all have the correct answers for the vocabulary-related questions, in order to prevent misunderstandings during the discussions. Teachers may refer to the Answers to Story Activities (which can be found on the website <www.oup.com/elt/teacher/readingcircles>), and answers can be checked quickly in class, either by each group writing several answers on the board, or by students reading their answers aloud to the class.

3 Remind students taking the role of Word Master to make a personal choice of significant words from the story, and not simply to choose words from the Word Focus activity.

Story Focus activities

1 These are designed to help students think about the theme and ideas of the story, and sometimes the stylistic devices used by the author. The exercises range from straightforward opinion questions, to exercises focusing on the significance of selected passages, and to creative activities such as writing a new ending for the story. All these will help students in their reader response – how they as individual readers react to and understand the story.

2 The Story Focus activities model the close reading required of students in their Role Sheet preparation. In most cases, there are no right or wrong answers to these activities, and students should be encouraged, not to look for answers 'approved by the teacher', but to explore their own ideas and responses. They are free to say and think whatever they like about a story – this freedom is part of the 'magic' of Reading Circles.

About the Authors

1 These are short biographies of the authors of the original texts, giving brief details of their lives, other books they may have written, and perhaps an anecdote or an interesting quotation.

2 Encourage students to read these biographies during their role preparation time as they may gain a useful perspective on the story from the author's life.

3 These short pieces can also be used as a starting point for students working on a project about authors. A mini-presentation or a poster session (see page 23) about an author's life can be an interesting way of extending the Reading Circles work after the group discussions. The short biographies in the book serve as good models of both the type of information to look for and the level of vocabulary to be used when creating a poster presentation.

The Bookworms Club
for Reading Circles

THE METALS SET		THE GEMS SET
	STAGES 5 and 6	◄ Bookworms Club *Diamond*
Bookworms Club *Platinum* ►	STAGES 4 and 5	◄ Bookworms Club *Ruby*
Bookworms Club *Gold* ►	STAGES 3 and 4	◄ Bookworms Club *Coral*
Bookworms Club *Silver* ►	STAGES 2 and 3	◄ Bookworms Club *Pearl*
Bookworms Club *Bronze* ►	STAGES 1 and 2	

The two sets of Bookworms Club books, *Metals* and *Gems*, offer different progressions through the Bookworms language stages.

The Metals Set starts at Stage 1 and moves at a gentler pace upwards through the levels to Stage 5. Each volume has five stories at the lower level and two stories at the higher level. The stories offer a wide variety of themes to interest young adults, and *The Metals Set* is an ideal starting point for students new to Reading Circles.

The Gems Set starts at Stage 2 and moves at a faster pace upwards through the levels to Stage 6. Each volume has four stories at the lower level and three stories at the higher level. This faster progression and the more mature thematic matter of the stories, many of which are taken from the *Bookworms World Stories* collections, are suitable for more advanced students.

BOOKWORMS CLUB
Stories for Reading Circles

THE METALS SET

BOOKWORMS CLUB BRONZE STAGES 1 AND 2

The Horse of Death by Sait Faik, from *Four Turkish Stories*
The Little Hunters at the Lake by Yalvac Ural, from *Four Turkish Stories*
Mr Harris and the Night Train by Jennifer Bassett, from *One-Way Ticket*
Sister Love by John Escott, from *Sister Love and Other Crime Stories*
Omega File 349: London, England by Jennifer Bassett, from *The Omega Files*
Tildy's Moment by O. Henry, from *New Yorkers*
Andrew, Jane, the Parson, and the Fox by Thomas Hardy, from *Tales from Longpuddle*

BOOKWORMS CLUB SILVER STAGES 2 AND 3

The Christmas Presents by O. Henry, from *New Yorkers*
Netty Sargent and the House by Thomas Hardy, from *Tales from Longpuddle*
Too Old to Rock and Roll by Jan Mark, from *Too Old to Rock and Roll and Other Stories*
A Walk in Amnesia by O. Henry, from *New Yorkers*
The Five Orange Pips by Sir Arthur Conan Doyle, from *Sherlock Holmes Short Stories*
The Tell-Tale Heart by Edgar Allan Poe, from *Tales of Mystery and Imagination*
Go, Lovely Rose by H. E. Bates, from *Go, Lovely Rose and Other Stories*

BOOKWORMS CLUB GOLD STAGES 3 AND 4

The Black Cat by Edgar Allan Poe, from *Tales of Mystery and Imagination*
Sredni Vashtar by Saki, from *Tooth and Claw*
The Railway Crossing by Freeman Wills Crofts, from *As the Inspector Said and Other Stories*
The Daffodil Sky by H. E. Bates, from *Go, Lovely Rose and Other Stories*
A Moment of Madness by Thomas Hardy, from *The Three Strangers and Other Stories*
The Secret by Arthur C. Clarke, from *The Songs of Distant Earth and Other Stories*
The Experiment by M. R. James, from *The Unquiet Grave*

BOOKWORMS CLUB PLATINUM STAGES 4 AND 5

No Morning After by Arthur C. Clarke, from *The Songs of Distant Earth and Other Stories*
The Nine Billion Names of God by Arthur C. Clarke, from *The Songs of Distant Earth and Other Stories*
Across the Australian Desert by Robyn Davidson, from *Desert, Mountain, Sea*
Casting the Runes by M. R. James, from *The Unquiet Grave*
The Songs of Distant Earth by Arthur C. Clarke, from *The Songs of Distant Earth and Other Stories*
Feuille d'Album by Katherine Mansfield, from *The Garden Party and Other Stories*
The Doll's House by Katherine Mansfield, from *The Garden Party and Other Stories*

BOOKWORMS CLUB
Stories for Reading Circles

THE GEMS SET

BOOKWORMS CLUB PEARL STAGES 2 AND 3

Callus by Janet Tay Hui Ching, from *Cries from the Heart: Stories from Around the World*

Dora's Turn by Jackee Budesta Batanda, from *Cries from the Heart: Stories from Around the World*

The Memento by O. Henry, from *New Yorkers*

The Cask of Amontillado by Edgar Allan Poe, from *The Pit and the Pendulum and Other Stories*

The Story-Teller by Saki, from *Tooth and Claw*

Breaking Loose by M. G. Vassanji, from *Dancing with Strangers: Stories from Africa*

The Silk by Joy Cowley, from *The Long White Cloud: Stories from New Zealand*

BOOKWORMS CLUB CORAL STAGES 3 AND 4

Gathering of the Whakapapa by Witi Ihimaera, from *The Long White Cloud: Stories from New Zealand*

The Waxwork by A. M. Burrage, from *A Pair of Ghostly Hands and Other Stories*

The Glorious Pacific Way by Epeli Hau'ofa, from *Playing with Fire: Stories from the Pacific Rim*

A Kind of Longing by Philip Mincher, from *The Long White Cloud: Stories from New Zealand*

Missiya, the Wild One by Vijita Fernando, from *Land of my Childhood: Stories from South Asia*

The Stepmother by Anne Ranasinghe, from *Land of my Childhood: Stories from South Asia*

Because of the Rusilla by Mena Abdullah & Ray Mathew, from *Doors to a Wider Place: Stories from Australia*

BOOKWORMS CLUB RUBY STAGES 4 AND 5

Carapace by Romesh Gunesekera, from *Land of my Childhood: Stories from South Asia*

A Devoted Son by Anita Desai, from *Land of my Childhood: Stories from South Asia*

The Intelligence of Wild Things by Chitra Banerjee Divakaruni, from *Land of my Childhood: Stories from South Asia*

Going Home by Archie Weller, from *Doors to a Wider Place: Stories from Australia*

My Oedipus Complex by Frank O'Connor, from *Treading on Dreams: Stories from Ireland*

Irish Revel by Edna O'Brien, from *Treading on Dreams: Stories from Ireland*

The Judge's House by Bram Stoker, from *Ghost Stories*

BOOKWORMS CLUB DIAMOND STAGES 5 AND 6

Millie by Katherine Mansfield, from *The Garden Party and Other Stories*

Her First Ball by Katherine Mansfield, from *The Garden Party and Other Stories*

Men and Women by Claire Keegan, from *Treading on Dreams: Stories from Ireland*

Mr Sing My Heart's Delight by Brian Friel, from *Treading on Dreams: Stories from Ireland*

Death Wish by Lawrence Block, from *American Crime Stories*

Cooking the Books by Christopher Fowler, from *The Fly and Other Horror Stories*

The Stolen Body by H. G. Wells, from *The Fly and Other Horror Stories*

Teacher Notes for Reading Circles

Role Badges

These role icons can be photocopied and then cut out to make badges or stickers for the members of the Reading Circle to wear.

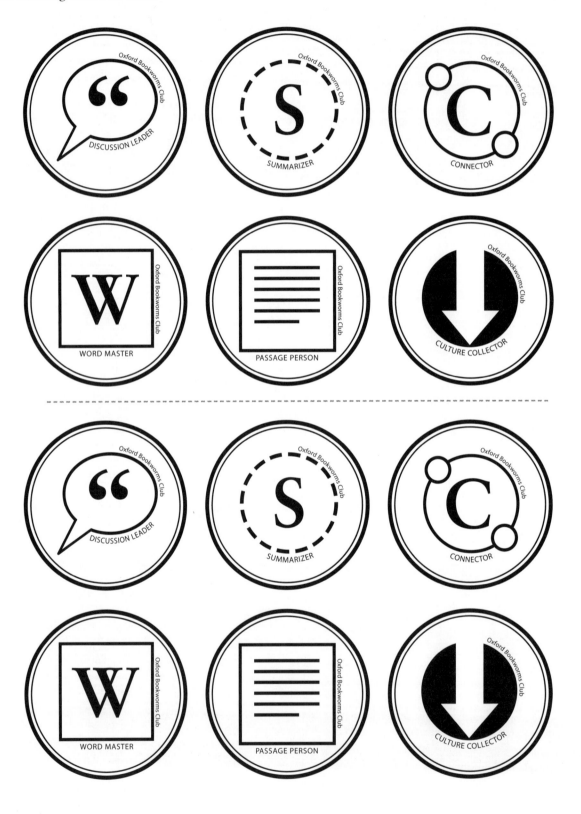